Themes from my Father

Janet Cantor Gari

Themes from My Father

Published in the USA by:
BearManor Media
PO Box 1129
Duncan, OK 73534-1129
www.BearManorMedia.com

ISBN-10: 1-59393-230-8
ISBN-13: 978-1-59393-230-5

Cover design and layout by Allan T. Duffin.

Printed in the United States of America

TABLE OF CONTENTS

DEDICATION

To Barack Obama

for making my father's most cherished dream come true

PREFACE

From the earliest time I can remember I have always been a liberal—or, as my daughter would say, a "fighting liberal." My father, for as long as he could remember, was a staunch Democrat, and he raised me and my sisters to stand up for what we believed in. We did. There didn't seem to be anything worse than occasional hot tempers between the political parties. The horrifying hatred we are now experiencing didn't seem to exist.

Yes, I'm highly opinionated, but I have always listened to opposing views. Today, however, it's impossible to pay attention to the sheer insanity and the bold lies of what used to be the Republican party.

What's going on?

CHAPTER ONE
In the Beginning

When I was born in 1927, the only "Hoover" I knew was a vacuum cleaner. I didn't know what a President was. Two years later came the stock market crash, and we were forced to move out of the lavish estate my father had acquired on Long Island. He was flat broke and owed $250,000. Always resourceful, he wrote two little books—*Caught Short* and *Yoo Hoo, Prosperity*. They sold like the proverbial hot cakes, and the debt was paid off to the penny.

My sisters were twelve, eleven, eight and six years older than I, but it didn't take long for me to become politically aware. Even my crayon drawings in kindergarten reflected the New Deal!

My father knew Al Smith and his progressive policies very well and supported him fully when he ran against Hoover. Although Smith had the backing of Tammany Hall, he was never beholden to them, but that and his being a Catholic doomed his campaign. It wasn't until John Kennedy that the country matured enough to trust a candidate to separate church and state.

I had always assumed that my father spoke disparagingly about Hoover because of the Great Depression, but as I grew older and began to read more than the assigned school books, I was at first confused about what could have been so bad about a man who tried to avoid the crash with public works, an increase in the top tax bracket and enlargement of corporate taxes. After World War I, he assembled and worked with organizations supplying food to war victims. He was all for regulating business practices, making home ownership possible for those who had never owned a home, and promoting health education. He was also in charge of the Mississippi Flood recovery.

Aye, there was the rub!

During the disaster black people were brutalized and prevented from leaving relief camps. Assistance that was meant for sharecroppers often found its way to the land owners instead. Black men, sometimes at gunpoint, were used as forced labor. Here, Hoover, the erstwhile humanitarian, not only did nothing to stop these egregious practices, but also suppressed the knowledge from becoming public by making a deal with the black leader, Robert Russa Moton (and shame on him, too!). If Moton kept quiet, Hoover, when elected President, would help the black people to his full capability. He lied. In fact, it was he who launched the "Southern Strategy" with which we are familiar today.

America had always been called "the melting pot" because of the various nationalities and religions of the immigrants who sought citizenship here. Actually, there was a "sub" melting pot called show business, in which everyone was indeed equal, and their native differences were good naturedly used as fodder for jokes and sketches. My father had many friends in show business, and we grew up with all kinds of people around the house—black and white, gay and straight, religious and non-religious, foreign and native born, etc. Oddly enough, I don't recall ever meeting an Asian person or a Native American. Perhaps this is because Hollywood usually made up white actors to play those roles, and my father didn't know any of the "extras" who were of the actual races. To say we were "color blind" would be ridiculous. Of course we could physically see if a person had black skin or bright red hair, but it simply registered on our brains the same as observing a moustache or blue eyes.

Our servants were also all made up of various nationalities and religions. They, too, were treated with the utmost respect; they were never considered inferior people just because they didn't have the skills or talent for more impressive jobs. There was one rule about which my father was adamant. He would not have a black servant. Having a black secretary was perfectly fine, but as he said, "I will never have a black person wait on me. I would be looking into Bert's face."

My father and Bert Williams met in the "Follies" playing "Pappy and Son." Both wore blackface, as Williams was light skinned. He was seventeen years older than my father and, unlike my father, was well educated and well read. They made each other laugh, and it developed into the most meaningful relationship my father ever had—except, of course, with my mother. My father always credited Williams with teaching him comedy timing and opening up a world of knowledge outside of show business. He felt Bert Williams was far superior to him in every way, and it was that analysis that shaped our entire outlook on life. Although my father was always a fighter for civil rights, he never dreamed we would one day have a black President. How thrilled he would have been, and I'm sure he would have considered it a personal tribute to his dear friend Bert Williams.

One New Year's Eve the cast was having a party at their hotel, a place where Williams was not allowed to register. My father made light of it and suggested that the two of them have their own party. One would bring the beer, and one would bring the sandwiches. He waited quite a while for Williams to arrive and asked what took him so long. Bert, now one of the biggest stars of the "Follies" of that year, explained that he had had a difficult time being allowed into my father's hotel, including having to take the service elevator.

"I wouldn't mind so much," Bert said, "if the applause weren't still ringing in my ears."

CHAPTER TWO
Franklin D. Roosevelt

Throughout my childhood and into my teens the words *President* and *Roosevelt* were synonymous. Even with all I knew about politics, I still somehow believed that it would always be the status quo—very much the way we feel our parents will always be there to protect us from life's hardships.

Schools were ultra-patriotic during the war, and I once innocently asked my father why, if we were the greatest country in the world, we didn't just take over all the other countries and make them like us. He explained the concept of imperialism to me. What a shame he couldn't have been around to explain it to Bush as well.

Although they were not as close as pals, my father and Roosevelt had known and admired each other when Roosevelt was Governor of New York, and after Roosevelt, despite being stricken with Infantile Paralysis, had been elected President, he called upon my father to inquire if he could round up ten millionaires to donate each year to an organization created to find a cure. My father remarked that this would be difficult to do, but paraphrasing *The March of Time*, the popular newsreel of the period, he suggested that having each and every man, woman and child donate ten cents, it could be called "The March of Dimes," and the funds would come in regularly.

"But where would they send it?" asked the President.

"You have a very nice address right here," said my father.

And so it happened, and my father lived long enough to see polio wiped out.

It was always ironic to me that George M. Cohan, a not-very-nice man who blatantly waved the flag for commercial purposes and showed himself to be anti-union, was made to look like an American icon in the movie *Yankee Doodle Dandy*. The great actor, singer and dancer, Jimmy Cagney, was so lovable that it all seemed true, while Cagney himself was an active liberal until the very end of his life when he became grumpy and conservative. In the earlier days, he and my father had been great friends.

Roosevelt, actually using many of the proposals Hoover had advocated, turned the country around. Medicare, Medicaid and Social Security were established, and once again we were on our way to prosperity.

Although he joked about it in movies and on radio, my father was proud to pay his 94% income tax because, as he said, "I'm grateful that I'm earning enough to owe it to the country that made it possible."

World War II, of course, provided many, many jobs, and Roosevelt was a courageous and successful Commander-in-Chief.

At one time, when my father was visiting the White House, the two men were discussing the plight of the Jews, and Roosevelt had tears in his eyes. I firmly believe those tears were genuine, but first and foremost he was a politician, and, considering the anti-Semitism and anti-immigration sentiments of both Congress and what he considered to be a majority of the people, he made no moves to save the refugees in dire need of help.

I didn't know about this until many, many years later, and it will always invoke a pang of hurt and disappointment.

CHAPTER THREE
Harry S. Truman

Roosevelt was prepared to have Henry Wallace on the ticket with him for the 1944 election, but he was advised that most of the country thought he was too far left and would damage the President's chances of re-election. He therefore picked the somewhat unknown Harry Truman, who became President when Roosevelt died mid term.

When he ran on his own in 1948, Truman, too, wanted the brilliant Mr. Wallace, but once again he was advised against that choice and selected Alvin Barkley. Every pundit was sure that Truman would be defeated by the Republican, Thomas E. Dewey—especially since Henry Wallace was running on a third-party ticket.

It was the first time I was able to vote (the voting age then being twenty-one), and I was very excited and eager to cast my ballot for Henry Wallace. Although my father liked him too, he strongly advised me not to split the vote by backing a third party.

"Wallace won't win," he said, "but neither will Truman, and we'll be stuck with Dewey." How right he was, and I'm glad I listened to him.

The State of Israel was just being established as a place of refuge for displaced Jews.

It was young, innocent and idealistic, not yet having political experience or maneuvers. The people turned desert into farmland and formed communities and educational opportunities. My parents were strong Zionists and visited the new State to raise money and contribute in any way they could. They brought boxes and boxes of toys for children who had never owned anything. My mother cried when she asked one little girl what she would like, and the child replied, "Love me."

Back home, traveling to Florida, my father was given a 60th birthday dinner as a fund raiser. Following his serious, appreciative speech was one given by President Truman—warm, funny and heartfelt. I was thrilled to have been there to hear it live.

Someone once asked me if I felt that Israel was my "homeland." I thought this was a ridiculous question. Of course not! America is my homeland. I've never even been to Israel, and I don't practice any religion. Today Israel is as complicated as any other foreign country, and I hope, like the rest of the world, that eventually a peaceful solution will be found.

CHAPTER FOUR
Walter Winchell

Around 1910, good looking and personable Walter Winchell, pursuing a career as my father did, joined a troupe of young song-and-dance performers, shepherded by Gus Edwards, called "The Newsboys Sextet." My father was to appear in Gus Edwards' "Kid Kabaret" in 1912. However, Winchell had very little talent and had to look elsewhere to make a name for himself. He was sly and smart and wrote for any newspaper that would have him, quickly rising to the top because of the bits of gossip he'd find with no pressure to check for facts. Eventually, he had the most widely read column in the country.

In his personal life, he left his wife and moved in with June Magee. Everyone assumed they were married, but he had never bothered to get a divorce from his wife. They had three children: two girls and a boy. Although June was extremely attractive and had a charming personality, Winchell was obsessed with their daughter Walda.

I went to school with Walda, a sweet, sad girl liked by all. In our third grade dramatic presentation, I even played Peter Pan to her Wendy! Her birthday party was a real shock to me. All the girls I knew, including myself, wore their one party dress, while the boys wore white shirts and jackets. We played the usual games, viewed the opening of presents and enjoyed ice cream and cake, taking home little baskets of goodies. Not Walda. Her party was held in a hotel ballroom with a full orchestra and a complete dinner served by the hotel waiters. The entertainment was strictly professional, and, to me, the most startling thing was that Walda wore a full-length evening gown, sewn, of course, to a child's proportions.

As Walda grew older, her father stopped at nothing to drive away any boyfriends in her life. The movie *The Sweet Smell of Success* was based on Winchell's fixation, but since he was still alive at the time the film was made, his character safely became a brother instead of a father. Walda's real-life brother committed suicide.

Power-hungry Walter Winchell branched out from his gossip column and acquired his own radio show, where he found red baiting, during the Cold War with Russia, paid off, and he cleared the way for the despicable McCarthy witch hunts.

CHAPTER FIVE
Dwight Eisenhower, Richard Nixon and Adlai Stevenson

Catchy slogans are very helpful to a campaign. "I Like Ike" was heard loudly all over America when the popular General ran for President in 1952. Another example is when my father ran for President as a publicity stunt on his radio show in the early Thirties, incorporating many of his cherished political beliefs in the song "When I'm the President." The musical phrase, "WE WANT CANTOR" became so popular that it followed him around for the rest of his career.

Eisenhower was not only a hero but also a good person, and there was much talk about the Democrats trying to persuade him to run on their ticket. He felt that he was a Republican, however, even though he was a moderate, and his accomplishments as President were laudable.

How did he end up with Richard Nixon as his running mate? All I knew about Nixon at that point was that I had been one of the protesters against the Mundt/Nixon bill, which required all communists to register with the government. This was aimed not only at those who wanted to overthrow the government (they would have been closely watched by the FBI in any case), but also to establish more power over free speech and, basically, private opinions.

I must interject that my father was disappointed that he was never called up by the House Un-American Activities Committee. He had many liberal friends, but had never known any one of them to be a communist (if they had been, the subject had never come up), and he was eager to tell off the Committee.

What a poor choice the Democrats made in nominating Stevenson! Our country is always looking for a Big Daddy, even if he's as doltish as Bush II. Although Stevenson had been married for over twenty years, he was divorced and could not supply a First Lady. (Horrors! Would our children grow up to think divorce was okay?) He was also an intellectual, and that meant he couldn't possibly be an "everyman." The deck was stacked.

CHAPTER SIX
The Kennedy Clan and the Aftermath

Gloria Swanson was the most beautiful woman I had ever seen in my very young life. Her violet eyes and perfect features made her look like an idealized painting, and I stared open-mouthed when my father introduced me to her and her little boy.

My father wanted to be a part of United Artists, which was formed as an independent film studio by some of the biggest stars of the day. Thus he became a friend of Miss Swanson, who was one of the founders.

Our family had begun to spend winters in New York, where my father would do stage work; and summers in California, where he would perform in movies. We lived in numerous summer rentals, and Gloria Swanson was our neighbor in one of them.

I was a small child and had no reason to give any thought to the Swanson boy's father, but as an adult I learned of the very open notorious affair between Swanson and Joseph P. Kennedy, and it was assumed that the little boy I had met was his son.

It turned out that all the Kennedy men followed in their father's footsteps as far as personal morality was concerned. Although the family prayed as strict Catholics and produced large broods of their own, the 7th commandment seemed to have been eliminated from their list of required behavior. In Chris Matthews' fascinating and illuminating book *Jack Kennedy—Elusive Hero*, he details their pattern of compartmentalizing their lives and their work.

John Kennedy was the youngest candidate ever to win the White House. The country had become youth oriented, and Big Daddy was now a daddy with whom the heads of young families could either identify with or emulate. Kennedy was immensely popular, as was his fashionable First Lady, and anyone from that era can remember exactly where he or she was when the announcement of his assassination rang out ominously over the airwaves.

Lyndon Johnson, his Vice President, had to be sworn in at once, so as not to leave the nation in shambles, and he soon accomplished many of Kennedy's proposals plus his own admirable advances for the country. He ran for President in the 1964 election and beat Barry Goldwater.

Too weak from heart disease and bedridden at this point, my father had already sent for his absentee ballot, but died before he could sign it, active to the end.

CHAPTER SEVEN
Richard Nixon and Gerald Ford

After accomplishing so many progressive policies for the country, Johnson unfortunately took the advice of his Defense Secretary, Robert McNamara, on the Vietnam war. Both of them later regretted it, but that didn't bring back the lives lost in that unpopular war. I was grateful that my son's draft number never came up. Johnson lost the next election to Richard Nixon.

I have to admit that I thoroughly disliked Nixon from the first time I saw him, when I went to Washington as a teenager to protest the Mundt/Nixon bill.

My father would have opposed him after thoroughly scrutinizing his policies and his career; but my mother, who had a keen intuition about people, would have immediately been concerned with his "shifty eyes."

Somehow the Watergate break-in did not come as a surprise. Nixon was already nicknamed "Tricky Dick," and indeed that he was. His "sincere" speech to try to save himself didn't work, and to avoid impeachment he resigned.

To add to the Republican shuffle, his Vice President, Spiro Agnew, had resigned because of his own impropieties. I knew this was serious business, but somehow Agnew made me laugh—like a comedic inept burglar. Gerald Ford was appointed to replace him. Ford was a genial fellow with conservative principles and a liberal wife, and although it was she who suffered from alcoholism, it was her clumsy husband who was often tripping and falling, taking much ribbing from the press. I must add that it was Betty Ford who will long be remembered—no, make that *honored*—for her immeasurable contributions to our society. She was more than a First Lady; she was a great lady.

Supposedly in an attempt to heal the country after the Watergate scandal, Ford immediately pardoned Nixon for "crimes which he committed or may have committed." This was a very unpopular decision, and the country did not agree with him. In a similar situation, there are many of us today who feel that even though President Obama issued no public statements about Bush and his cohorts, there should have been a reckoning.

CHAPTER EIGHT
Jimmy Carter

President Carter was and is a good man. When we use the expression "holier than thou," we usually refer to people who look down their noses at the rest of us and consider themselves superior. I believe Carter really was holier than so many of us, and I mean that in a context of admiration. He was never a hypocrite like the politicians who want us to believe they are personally in touch with God, who is the Being guiding their agendas. Carter simply followed the ethical principles of his faith as a matter of course.

I think my father would have thought of Carter as being similar to Will Rogers, the famous humorist and performer, in his philosophy and viewpoints. He did indeed have the wisdom, but not the wit. Unlike the other businessmn turned politician, his demeanor was completely different from the feisty Harry Truman. This time around the U.S. had not found Big Daddy but a kindly uncle they foolishly neglected to re-elect.

While successfully battling the energy shortage, Carter was also concerned with the environment, and his accomplishment in foreign affairs included the SALT II treaty. To me his greatest achievement was creating the Department of Education. I remember how important schooling was to my father, who never got past the sixth grade. He told us how W.C. Fields, well known for his comedy and his drinking (though never onstage), literally carried a trunk full of books with him when they were on the road. He not only insisted that my father read every one, but tested him on them!

I rather doubt that Jimmy Carter felt every kid needed a comic to follow him around, but he did feel that an education provided a good start in life.

It's hard to believe that there are politicians today who have no understanding of the correlation between education or training and job possibilities.

Next: an actor makes his entrance.

CHAPTER NINE
The Teflon President

Having tea with Governor and Mrs. Ronald Reagan was not one of the highlights of my life. They had come to a one-man show of my husband's paintings in a Beverly Hills gallery and bought one of the larger ones, inviting us to see where it was hanging in their home. I cannot imagine why we received this invitation—perhaps out of deference to my father, a fellow actor who had also been president of the Screen Actors Guild about fifteen years before Reagan was? When Nancy Reagan became First Lady of the United States, she was on the cover of *Time* magazine, posing, by chance, in front of my husband's painting—a plus for him but not for our country.

Tea time was awkward for me and my husband. We were trying to keep the conversation as far away from politics as possible and just be the polite benefactors of patrons of the arts. This was particularly difficult when Reagan questioned us about our life in New York. Although we would have been classified as middle-class, we lived in a neighborhood that was rapidly becoming impoverished, and the implication of Reagan's remarks was not to help the poor but rather to dump them somewhere else and thus clean up the area.

This was a far cry from the New Deal Democrat he had been when he joined the Army Air Corps in 1942. It was there—although mostly because he was involved with Nancy Davis, a minimally talented actress with strictly conservative views—that he did a complete turnaround and switched to being a Republican through and through.

During the time Reagan was in uniform, it was both popular and patriotic for movie stars to open their homes on weekends to soldiers on leave. It was also considered a duty to pick up hitchhiking military men and give them a lift whenever possible. One of my neighbors in New York related to me that when he was on leave in Los Angeles, where he had never been, he was thumbing a ride from one area to another, and who should stop to pick him up but Jane Wyman. He was so thrilled to be meeting a real movie star that he forgot where he was going, so she suggested that he come home with her, where he'd find a barbecue and a swimming pool. Reagan, then her husband, was anything but gracious. He growled at her for having added another guest and barely acknowledged the eager young soldier.

It certainly wasn't like that at our house, where EVERYONE was inolved!

As an actor, Ronald Reagan was only a mildly talented but very good-looking contract player. He and Jane Wyman made a cute couple, but it was she who went on to become a really fine actress and win an Academy Award. Reagan was always associated with two lines from two movies. He didn't win any awards, because it was the writing that was brilliant, not his acting. In *King's Row* he's remembered for asking, "Where's the rest of me?" in a shocking scene with an actor-proof line. In *Knute Rockne* he had the line "Win one for the Gipper," and he was nicknamed the Gipper forever after—once again because of a line from a script.

Playing the part of President was the only outstanding acting he ever did. Where Carter's personality had been too bland for a movie-struck nation, Reagan, still good-looking and able to read lines effectively, did a great deal of harm and smoothly got away with it. He slashed money for the poor and for student grants, broke the Air Traffic Controllers union and invented "trickle down" economics, to name a few of his "accomplishments." Today's Republicans never mention the fact that he raised taxes eleven times or that he left us with the biggest deficit ever.

I personally cannot praise his son, Ron Reagan, enough. Not only are his political views completely opposite of those of his parents, but he exudes real warmth—not the phony camaraderie of President Reagan. He always speaks respectfully of his father and seems to be devoid of any bitterness about things long past—like Ronald and Nancy's disdain for his career as a ballet dancer, when he was a really talented member of the second Joffrey Ballet Company.

Praise and encouragement from a parent are so important. My own father gave us lots of affection and emotional support, but he never took us seriously regarding a career. When I first started writing music, I was studying with a classical composer, and I would go into one of those RECORD YOUR VOICE studios and play every one of my early compositions on the available piano, sending the discs to my sister Margie, who helped me to pay for them. I have no idea if either of my parents ever heard them, because they never mentioned it, and I was too embarrassed to ask.

That certainly wasn't a pattern for George H. W. Bush. He obviously endowed even his totally befuddled son with enough self-esteem to win the Presidency, but that's another story.

CHAPTER 10
Clinton Outshines 1000 Points of Light

Although George H. W. Bush had an excellent military record and a comprehensive foreign policy, his typically Republican economic philosophy was not working at all. Along came Bill Clinton, and the country was ready for this charismatic, energetic and positive thinking young man. Unfortunately he was also a garden-variety skirt chaser, and his hypocritical opponents tried desperately to use it to their advantage. In our house my folks had never gossiped about anyone's personal life, and I felt that this situation was like one big gossip column.

From the very start this should have been a matter between Clinton and his wife. It had nothing whatsoever to do with politics, but I was angry with him for his arrogance in making no effort to be discreet, when he was smart enough to know the Republicans would be after his hide, and we really needed him in the White House.

After all the *sturm und drang* was over, however, he went on to win a second term, because he was the best thing to happen to the country, and most people recognized that fact.

Need a list? More peace and economic stability than any time in history. Lowest unemployment since the industrial revolution. Lowest inflation in thirty years. Not only tackled the deficit, but left us with a surplus! Strengthened NATO. Worked to stop drug trafficking around the world. I could go on and on and on.

As for "Don't ask, don't tell," he was trying to eliminate all obstacles for gay men and women in the military, but the only way he could get anywhere at all was to compromise his bill. It wasn't to his liking, but it was the best he could do at that time, and look how long it took to set things right.

Even as an adult I was at first inclined to shrug at gay issues, having grown up with a "who cares how other people live their lives? It's none of our business" perspective.

Then it became clear that the "other people" were being hurt—attacked, in fact—and it became my business. It was hard for me to understand why someone's lifestyle should threaten anyone else unless there was violence involved;

and the violence, both verbal and physical, came from the critics, not the participants.

I know my father would be proud at how far we've come as a nation, but we still have such a long way to go. It was tough to say goodbye to Bill Clinton and naïve of us not to realize just how bad things could get with the next administration, but this time the country wanted "a guy you could have a beer with"—or, in Dubya's case, at least a six-pack.

CHAPTER ELEVEN
Beating around the Bush

Let's face it: Awkward George Dubya was never our President; Cheney was. At the time, with thanks to Oscar Hammerstein for his perfect setup (dialect deliberate for *Show Boat*), I did what my father always used to do: I wrote a parody.

There's an ol' man in the Oval Office,
Fillin' the Chief with his good advice:
Give a few cents to some schools and health care
Long as the rich get a bigger slice.

Ol' man Cheney, dat ol' man Cheney,
He runs the country, cause Bush ain't brainy,
And ol' man Cheney, he jes keeps rollin' along.

He don't find weapons o' mass destruction,
But his fear tactic is shrewd deduction,
So ol' man Cheney, he jes keeps rollin' along.

You and me, we sweat and strain,
Tryin' our damnedest to make it plain:
Listen, folks, the war'll fail.
(You get a little spunk and you land in jail)
Ah gets weary and sick o' tryin'
Ah'm tired of Bush "savin'" me from dyin',
Yet ol'man Cheney, he jes keeps rollin' along.

Bush might have just slid by in spite of his gaffes, ignorance and Palinesque remarks, but 9/11 gave Cheney his big chance. He maneuvered us (and Bush) into a spurious war, lied about the reason and about the torture, which he seemed to relish and has said he would approve again.

The country was kept in a state of alarm with various and colorful "alerts," and Bush, who had the most unchallenging opportunity to capture or kill Osama Bin Laden, actually said publicly that he really wasn't interested. If that had fit into Cheney's plans, action would have been taken immediately, but Cheney was thriving on his power, accomplishing more behind the scenes than he would have as the elected President.

When it came to a second term, we were warned that it was only Bush who was keeping us safe, and no one was noting what was happening to our economy—just as people like my father never anticipated the stock market crash in 1929.

Leaving us in debt up to our ears and still fighting unpopular wars, good ol' Dubya trotted off to his ranch to attempt, literally, to rewrite history. He wasn't really a bad guy. He was more like a small child being given a chemistry set meant for college kids and playing with it without any adult supervision.

CHAPTER TWELVE
Yes, We Can

Oh, how I wish my parents and all my sisters could have been alive for Obama's election! Mother would have ordered a platter of deli sandwiches, and Margie would have made several batches of brownies (using Edna's fabulous recipe, of course!). There would have been a huge pot of coffee and several bottles of soda, and we would have been glued to the television watching the results, shouting as each report got better and better.

We would have booed the image of McCain and applauded the Obama posters; and when victory was finally announced, we would have been hugging each other and probably shedding a few tears of joy.

But they were no longer here and had no way of knowing.

Obama was not just my choice; he was (and is) someone I really believe in. I felt bad about his unrealistic dream of bipartisanship and wish he could have come in like a bulldozer, since he had both the Senate and the House; but even with McConnell's open admission that the entire Republican agenda was simply to make Obama a one-term President, he has managed to see that millions of people now have health insurance, to save the auto industry and thus protect millions of jobs, to get rid of prejudical treatment of those in the military, to protect women's rights and to accomplish many other things.

It was under his leadership that Bin Laden was finally annihilated, which is hardly a minor note!

So much more could have been achieved if it had not been for the Republican filibusters. I don't recall anything like this in my entire life of voting—nor do I ever remember such deep-seated hatred. I guess I didn't want to believe that race had anything to do with Obama's merciless opposition, but the bigots' coded messages are now so easy to decode.

Here's hoping we move forward, not backward.

CPSIA information can be obtained at www.ICGtesting.com
Printed in the USA
LVOW01s1145010813

345764LV00003B/212/P

9 781593 932305